When There Are No More Tears: *a Buddha's story of love*

By Victoria L. Johnson, Ph.D.

Published 2013 by:

McIntosh & Shobey Associates, Ltd.

http://mcintoshandshobeyassociates.weebly.com

Printed in the United States of America

ISBN: 978-0-9769868-3-6

Contents

With Devotion:

This book is dedicated to my deceased parents (James and Lucille), my children (Yamani, Kente, and Jasmine), my mentors in faith (Stevee, Helen, Michael and Valarie), my friends (too numerous to list), my siblings (Saundra and James), to my husbands (Prentiss, Willie, and Clarence), my Wizard (James), my editor and publicist (C.R. Toliver), Alyce and Enola, posthumously to Aunts, (Livey, Cornelia, Ruth), grandparents (Robert, Elizabeth, Vivian, Jason and Everett) and to a host of people who cheered me on and allowed me to read this book to them chapter by chapter as each was edited throughout the years, including Useni, Terri and Eloise. My constant loving four legged companions, Myoho, Abigail, and Sankofa listened to me when no one else could.

I thank all of those who wished me well and loved me as well as those who found supporting me an impossibility. Without everyone this story could never have been.

This book is also dedicated to anyone who has ever loved a child.

Foreword

Many books have shared how the power of faith helped an author turn their life or situation around. Most recently, the self help/awareness gurus, the pundits and prophets who guide our search for the Spiritual Grail of self reformation have successfully captured an audience for "The Secret", "The New Earth"…and the medical intuitives have reiterated the mind-body connection.

This is a story of how challenges afforded opportunities to deepen faith in Buddhism in order to create some value while solving seemingly impossible temporary problems resulting from karmic challenges. By karma I mean that all of my challenges were resultant from choices I made of my own free will and from life tendencies I brought with me at birth. If these facts were true then it was likewise my own responsibility to recognize, resolve and empower my own life. That was and remains no one else's responsibility.

"Many view Buddhism as a religion of quiet contemplation, best practiced apart from the stresses of society. Buddhas came to be depicted as serene static figures, aloof from the mundane worries of the world. But the historical Buddha, Shakyamuni (also known as Siddhartha Gautama) exerted himself tirelessly to talk with people." ("Living Buddhism", December 2012, p. 16)

My story is not about external peace, serenity, or separation from events in the external world (or even constant internal peace) for my practice of Buddhism is not of a sect that promotes ascetic practices. Quite the contrary I joined a sect that teaches that our "earthly desires equal enlightenment" and that: "A Buddha is not a supernatural being but an ordinary person who is enlightened to the external and ultimate truth that is the reality of all things, and who leads others to attain the same enlightenment". ("Living Buddhism", December 2012, p. 3)

In fact, I joined an organization that promotes the understanding that all living beings possess the Buddha nature no matter what the inner character or external circumstances. We can say it's him, it's her, it's them, it's this, and it's that. In the beginning and in the end, it all boils down to "karma" and a "Buddha" is but an ordinary human being who becomes "aware" of this. Karma. We come with it, create and expiate more of it as we live our lives.

No one escapes the struggles and hardships of life; thus, just understanding the law of cause and effect helps one to change "poison" into medicine.

"It is not what happens to us but how we respond to what happens to us that makes all the difference." Most importantly no matter what, one must be mindful of how we reach the goal! Process matters.

I had to burrow within adversities and challenges to discover my own truth. Was that "truth" always there or did it emerge after I had been immersed or bathed in challenge upon challenge upon challenge? There is no one exactly like me; likewise, choices that I made were exactly my own. Although similar, no two stories are the same.

The human preference to avoid pain while enjoying all of the pleasure makes this journey one that some readers would want to blame on someone or something outside of me. Seeking an external cause would have been such an easy thing to do. I chose, instead to interpret it as what it was.... my karma.

I had to grow to understand that my fears and weaknesses could only be used to liberate me if I wrestled with them and not with someone or something external to me.

Without judgment this is simply a personal story of choices that were made. Each of us can examine the choices of others with some commentary, and likewise others can comment on our choices. The greater challenge is to acknowledge and take responsibility for our choices. We cannot address what we cannot see nor understand as our "fundamental darkness", the origin of human delusions and a powerful source of suffering, without "lessons".

This book is Part One of journal entries collected over a twenty-five year period. Part Two is picked up in a sequel entitled: "Cattle Drive: the relationship safari".

Chapter One: Surrender

Perhaps more than anything else I felt that the last thing the world needed was one more book on a relationship that fell apart...so I hesitated for years about sharing my own story. The journal I kept for over twenty-five years was filled with my reference points, reporting the foolishness, vulnerabilities, fears, and foibles that evolved until I left an old world and discovered anew.

At times I became so absorbed by my story that I lost any ability to see that it might possess some relevance for anyone outside the drama that was mine. My children and musings and honest awareness for what I had been through provided the sense of purpose that had justified another day. Little else captured my attention, which was engulfed by the daily tasks at hand.

I spent years hoarding myself rather than to risk finding, falling, and failing again. I spent years reading, riding, walking, meditating, mothering, nurturing, and developing (because of all of it)...a spiritual side.

I focused on expectations for the future and the grit it took to muster and master another day; yet all the while I did battle to expel any pity for the past, the circumstances, the children, or myself. Gradually thoughts of the past slipped away. The deliberate choices that I made and self-renewal washed over and under and through the evolution of the woman I had been until I reinvented myself and became the woman who time and circumstances unveiled.

Rather than to be drowned by them I dove into the deep-water challenges that beckoned. Never choosing the easiest paths, I took the bold and risky steps that made the days and weeks and months and years melt into one long seam of time until I had raised the three children who had all been under the age of five when marriage to their father disintegrated.

Every step from the first had brought us closer to the fork in the road that was ultimately unavoidable. It would be so easy to blame someone, but blame was the one thing I could be sure this was definitely not about. Hadn't we seen our differences before the altar? Sure we had, yet we had gambled on the impossible becoming possible…. that the other one would change.

The disintegration of this relationship was an inevitable conclusion to what had repeatedly revealed polarized objectives. The principles, philosophies, strategies, and methods employed revealed limitations. Like trains traveling on parallel tracks, no collision was mandatory, but likewise neither was a lifelong partnership.

Our orbits increasingly never grazed the separate tracks and so in time it seemed an un-avoidable compromise, an impossible negotiation. It was a choice between each pursuing the lives we came here to live or one being compromised for the sake of the other. So one day we simply called it off. One morning he left.

What had simply been "about us" not only involved us. Eleven years, four degrees, four car notes, student loans, a mortgage and three children later it was just over. After a decade of striving, we two Ivy League trained professionals had "arrived". But when we arrived we shared no satisfaction for the destination. Each step towards our destination had taken us toward the void that emerged between us.

A valley, a gulf, and a distance that precluded interaction between orbits that no longer related to or depended upon one another...if they ever did. All illusions of any common sense of purpose had slipped away until that day when the compelling emptiness pushed us apart and we found ourselves not only separating, but in time headed towards divorce.

Having "it" all and yet having nothing that mattered had created, at least in me, anguish and agony, and a seething pain that seared my soul. The pain of "settling" for less than what could be just didn't ever seem a missing factor, but instead a constant one.

Staying together would require another decade or at the very least years of one or perhaps even both of us ceasing to exist and the pretense had reached its end.

The morning he left, he stood in the doorway and announced: "I am leaving and I'm not coming back." I looked at him and felt like running to get a pen and paper before asking him to put that pledge in writing in case he changed his mind, but I just stood there.

We had just had enough…of one another. Here I was living in Chicago and remembering how he had promised me that was a city we didn't have to move to. He wasn't off track. I was. Far away from my career goals and closer to his, I was the one whose train had derailed a long time ago. His goals and identity were intact and I was the one wondering more and more everyday who the hell was staring back at me when I looked in the mirror.

I dressed the children and like "normal" dropped them each at school and returned home and waited until it was time to retrieve them all. I sat on the steps between the first and second floor for hours and just stared.

That was the day it began. The day one future of possibilities was summarily executed. The day that ushered in realities of a future entirely unforeseen, bereft of logic and reason; yet fresh and filled with an authenticity that the routine of pretense in my former life never smelled of. I wondered what to expect from the life that was on the other side of this choice.

It was not just that he was leaving, but that I had put all my eggs in his basket. I had completely surrendered myself to his control and now there I was with three small children to feed, no job, no family and our "friends" were actually his associates. I was even living in "his" town.

Unwise by every practical measure, I had traded a chance for financial security for my sanity and with it the prospective sanity of my children. Unsure, uncertain, unsafe, I did what I only know to do. I wrote. I wrote that inside of this pain and rite of passage my spirit would thrive on its expectation that one day my fears, uncertainty, insecurity, and doubts would step aside while I resumed control of my life.

The days, the weeks, and even the years flowed each into the other until the day when I admitted the possibility that it was finally over.

An agonizing, collectively traumatizing metamorphosis became threads of the tapestry, and the adhesive for the mosaic that had been created by the milestones and markers of the journey from onset to completion.

Here and there, now and then I transferred the sadness within my heart to paper throughout the seamless moments that defined the twenty years it took to raise the children who were 1, 3, and nearly five, the day he left. Then it took another five years to collect my tattered soul to renew itself.

Never excluding even a comma, a sigh, a moment, or a quotation that became the story to transport me across this sea of suffering, one day I realized that the wounds would heal.

One day…there would be no more tears.

Chapter Two: In The Beginning Was the Word

How had it all begun? A glance from across a crowded, dim, and funky college dance floor launched a union between two lonely souls with independent interests and mutual desires.

Desirous of companionship, the "American" dream, and accomplishments, it was easy for us to lock into a purpose.

He had watched me from afar during my three year courtship with a classmate. While we were dancing he said he was "sorry" to hear we had broken up and then he snickered, "well not really, I am kinda glad you are single again."

"Oh yeah? Why? Are you interested in me?" Leave it to the brutal honesty of a Sagittarian to say exactly what was on my mind. Little did I know I was talking to another Sagittarian. So we danced and visited the punch bowl and talked and danced and visited the punch bowl and danced and talked.

I drove classmates from Wheaton to the party at Wellesley, but had already told everyone before we left that they might have to find their own way home. Who knows who we would each meet; so why get locked into transportation hurdles?

Hours later when the night was coming to a close he offered to walk me to my car only for us both to discover I had a flat tire. I think about four guys jumped at the chance to change the tire so the two of us continued to talk off to the side.

He said he thought I was amazing and wanted to give me a call. I said: "well if I give you this number and you don't call, I will NOT be calling you." He laughed. He called.

The next weekend he was visiting. He brought a candle, a book of poetry, a bottle of wine and music.

We put a blanket on my dormitory room floor, turned off the lights, lit the candle while the music played and he read the poetry.

We talked for hours and hours and hours until we both got sleepy. I told him, "we can cuddle and that's it. Understand?" We cuddled.

From there, it was on. Either I was with him on the weekends or he was with me. Museums, movies, campus lectures/events/parties, night clubs, long walks and talks… we enjoyed spending time together and enjoyed no longer being alone. He rejuvenated my social life, which had been in the crapper since the break up with my boyfriend and he admired the image of the couple he had seen. Now he was the matching puzzle piece.

He was a senior at Harvard and I was a senior at Wheaton. The travel from Norton to Cambridge, Massachusetts was about a forty-five minute drive and leaving campus for the weekends meant we got to focus on school work during the week while saving time for fun on the weekends.

He knew he was going to medical school and I was unsure of my next move. I had come to college as pre-med and painfully realized after sophomore year that I was more interested in love than isolated devotion to pre-medical studies so I had switched to

Urban Studies. A scholarship from The Experiment in International Living had allowed me to spend two months in Brazil between sophomore and junior year which sparked an interest in Latin America. Returning to Brazil for a year, perhaps as a volunteer in the Peace Corps was an option I was considering, but I was flexible.

Things became more serious. My mom was especially excited to know I was dating someone who was pre-med. I was just happy to be dating.

We met in September and before the end of the first semester, the fairy tale began to unravel. Once when he missed his bus back to Cambridge I gave him my car keys and told him to drive safely and I would take the bus in the next weekend. I never thought about asking about the car. When he got back we talked by phone as usual, but when I came to visit him the following weekend he told me that while driving back it had rained so hard that my car was difficult to drive so he pulled over, parked it on the side of the road and hitch hiked into Cambridge.

"You left my car on the side of the road a week ago and didn't think to tell me?!" I called a few friends who took me to the car and there it was stripped to the core. The leather seats were missing, the doors were off. This was a Renault 4, a French car which they no longer even made and every part on it would have been in high demand.

I had worked two summers and two semesters to squirrel away enough money to buy the car. His response: "Well, it wasn't a fancy car anyway!"

I thought well, maybe it's gone because something better will come along. Yeah, why be so hung up on a 'car'!

During the semester break I was invited to Chicago to meet his family. During dinner I noticed that he, his brother, and his father were all talking to one another but no one was talking to the mother. The three way conversation excluded both me and her so I started talking to her. At some point he turned to me and said, "Oh you don't have to feel that you have to talk to her, we don't." I just replied, "Okay but I think I will anyway."

What tha....?

I think the yellow "caution" lights were blinking and the red stop signs were starting to appear, but in my typical "never say die" attitude, I ignored them all.

Nobody is perfect, right? There were probably things about me and my family that seemed a little odd, too, so what's the big deal? No matter what happens the important thing is to accept people as they are, right?

So we kept dating and then one day that word popped up: marriage. What did I think about it? He said he thought it would be great but he just had not met the perfect girl and my ego stood right up as I said, what do you mean?! "I AM the perfect girl" and that's how the journey invoking the "word" began.

Chapter Three: To Have and To Hold

After three and a half years I had started to consider that my marriage was a mistake. I was unhappy. Although I had wanted to wait until I finished my Masters degree, my fiancé had insisted that we marry the second summer after our college graduation. It bothered me that we hadn't been able to put our heads together enough to even attend Graduate Schools in the same cities. How would we make compromises in a marriage?

In addition, I was more than a little troubled by his reaction to my acceptance to Johns Hopkins. As we were completing college and it was time to apply to graduate schools I hesitated until the last minute but then discovered a program in international affairs at Johns Hopkins. Although he had applied to Harvard Medical School I suggested he apply to Johns Hopkins, too. When I got my acceptance letter to Johns Hopkins I asked if he had heard from Hopkins about his application and without a pause he said, "No and I won't because I never applied. I never expected you to get in. How did that happen anyway?"

I didn't think "he doesn't believe me". I thought "what a sense of humor". My entire life had been a course in miracles....doing what others deemed impossible. Clearly his position was just funny.....or so I thought at the time.

Besides, I thought well time will tell. I will start my two year Master's Degree program in Washington, D.C. while he stays in Cambridge, Massachusetts and if it's real it will last and if it's not it won't. I didn't worry much about which outcome would prove the test of time. I said to myself....how interesting.

One year later he was still talking marriage while living in separate cities and that even though we would start out our marriage living in separate cities, our time apart would be great for our grades and we would have the personal satisfaction of having launched a marriage together. I was still thinking...how interesting.

College senior year had been one of closure.... ending four years of liberal arts studies, etc. My classmates at this all girls' college seemed to be getting engaged and I had felt that I needed the same in order to make my "closure" complete.

I had felt this unspoken peer pressure to pin down a partner. Marriage now was not his idea. It was now mine. I pressed for the engagement, but almost the moment after I got the ring I questioned marriage-or at least so soon, and to one another. Now he was pushing for the next step, the final step, the unchangeable step. His reasoning seemed about as convoluted as mine had been when I pressed for the engagement. I think that was that "be careful for what you wish for because you just might get it" moment.

To make matters worse, while he was planning a wedding for the following summer, I was planning a research project in Brazil that would last from the week after the end of spring semester until a week before the fall semester would begin. There was no time for a wedding!! Besides, who would plan it all?

Then he said he would handle every detail in cooperation with my mother. I could fly back from Brazil, dress for the wedding, and we would spend five days "honeymooning" together (in his Harvard dormitory room) and then dash off to complete the second year of my master's degree program at Johns Hopkins in Washington, D. C.

I thought to myself, is he for real? Not knowing whether to be flattered or frightened. I said, "Okay, let's think about it."

After college graduation we were living in separate cities and he had come to visit. One night he wouldn't stop. For two hours all I heard was that he thought he was flunking out of med school and it was all because of missing me. He would lose me unless we got married. The distance between Boston and Washington, D.C. was "bad" for the engagement. We had to get married. I kept saying that I wasn't saying no to marriage, I was saying, let's wait. He kept saying, "To wait is to say no!" On and on and on and on he went until I said, "For Christ's sake, plan your stupid wedding." He looked at me and said, "You won't regret it." I did...from the start until the very end; but a commitment is a commitment, right?

As planned I left for Brazil, but three days before I was to leave Brazil and return for the wedding I called my folks to say that I didn't want to get married. I had changed my mind. Since I was bi-lingual I had an offer from the First National Bank of Brazil and wanted to accept it. My father told me that I should plan to live there forever if I missed the wedding and wasted the thousands of dollars he had spent on the entire affair.

I rushed from my research project in Brazil and dressed for the wedding. My groom handed me the vows he had written for us and I marched down the aisle to the music and kaleidoscope of slides he had assembled to tell the world "our story" as he saw it.

I kept thinking this is a scene from a bad dream, and when I wake up it will be over. The only thing that I had done for the wedding was to buy my dress, which was black. I thought my message was clear and that a gallant knight would rush into the hall riding a marvelous horse, rescue me before the vows and save me from this doomsday activity I had agreed to.

The knight never came.

When the wedding ended, we went to the reception. Receptions are seductive. The people who have loved and nurtured and admired you for a lifetime are wishing you well, pouring out your praises and precious stories that would inspire the dead to rise. You are cuddled. You are pampered. You are the centerpiece. Everything revolves around you. Who wouldn't enjoy the attention, the smiles, and the tears? Our parents had paid for our wedding night at a luxury hotel for the evening. We didn't make love.

At 3 a.m. I started crying and thinking I've made a grave mistake. I kept rewinding the scenes from the day on my mental video. Wasn't it odd that out of hundreds of guests at the wedding I could count his friends and family with fingers from both hands and still have fingers left over. Didn't he have more friends? Where was the rest of his family? Did I know who I had married? Who HAD I married? I turned over to look at him in bed and found him staring. He asked, "Why are you crying? I said, "I feel that this wedding may have been a mistake." "Jitters", he said and turned his back.

My mom was pretty happy. Both of her girls would be married to guys who would be doctors! My dad was pretty happy that both of his girls were married, period! He and my mom had gone to City Hall to get married and college and graduate school were what he perceived of as just a waste of time-especially for girls. He had no problem telling me that he was glad he had married me off before I got too many degrees to price myself out of the market. No harm intended. That was just his point of view. He meant no harm and I took no offense. He didn't know how much school meant to me and at the time neither did I.

Since we were newlyweds and students, my folks paid for my airfare and his parents paid for his. We spent several days in his Harvard dormitory room and then I returned to grad school. I shrugged it all off and refused to think about it. We talked by phone and visited bimonthly. The first semester of my second year wasn't over before he called me saying, "You have to leave your program. I'm flunking out of medical school. I'm too depressed about your absence. A wife should be with her husband. We shouldn't be separated. I can't concentrate with you so far away. No matter what job or career you choose, I will always be the primary breadwinner of our family because as a doctor I will earn more than you. You need to be here to help me finish medical school."

On and on and on and on he went with each call. While I was thinking it over, I started to receive depressing letters and copies of his low-test scores.

My guilt was rising and I compromised. Two months later I agreed to leave my program. He rented a van, came to town and we moved in together. My professors were supportive and I could finish from afar.

As a Proctor, he had been awarded living space that was smaller than my apartment but we squeezed my furniture in and I began my new job of helping him get through medical school.

I took over the lion's share of his responsibilities as Proctor…. after all we classified as "Married Proctors". The details don't really matter but I gradually pitched in with anything and everything that would free him to just concentrate on medical school.

One source of his income was a job he could do any time he chose without supervision. It wasn't long before he asked me to do that job while he reported the results. This then was added to my plate. I had moved the first of the year and before long it was Spring. Everywhere I went, people smiled at me and said what a happy couple we seemed to be. Few people had a helpmate.

Suddenly for the second time within six months I was packing up everything again after he announced we would be moving to an apartment. About the same time I received the great news that I had been accepted to the doctoral program at Tufts in Political Science.

We moved and I started my doctoral program with a full scholarship, stipend, work-study, and Teaching Assistantship. I was barely finished with enjoying my "saved by the bell" moment when he said to me one day, "You know I was thinking that with the extra income you are bringing in we could buy a car and a home stereo system." Marriage is about sharing openly and unselfishly, right?

We got a loan for a car and he selected a stereo system. When the salesman rang up the system I cringed but thought, maybe he needs the music to calm down after a stressful day at school so just suck it up. My graduate program was a significant commute, but I had problems ever getting the car and he preferred that I not bother the stereo since he thought it especially irritating when he rushed home to relax and found the stations or records changed. Ever play that game of maybe I can touch it, change it, and then return it to its original setting before he/she gets in? Not fun.

Time passed and we were increasingly living separate lives. Of course, with my Ph.D. program I was able to keep busy…to avoid focusing on loneliness or feelings of being neglected. With his erratic 24-hour "on call" schedule it just got to be easier to leave each other notes and messages about the honey do's… "Honey do this. Honey do that."

It got so I would create events or schedule dinner parties at our place just to make sure that I could share a meal or evening with him. Guests thought we were the perfect couple because on these occasions I would be so "touchy-feely" or all over him. I started working at being someone he felt more motivated to come home to. Lots of our social life was actually obligatory…like dinners with senior professors or physicians. As students we were often invited to annual dinner parties in their elegant homes. When he felt the need to coach me on what to wear, what to say, what not to wear, what not to say, how much to talk and when not to.... I realized that the long periods of absence were taking their toll. It wasn't about me so much as the roles I was expected to fulfill...you know, the image.

Most wives were the breadwinners while their husbands attended medical school. For a few couples both husband and wife attended medical school. Most hosts seemed totally charmed by my dinner conversations but he worried (and expressed it to me often) that I might be making the other wives feel "bad" by talk of global politics.... which was my field of study.

No matter, for eventually, there were too many lonely hours to fill after class work, housework, the job, and his tasks were finished. To fill in hours I began to write, publish and go deeper into preparing my dissertation. I increasingly wondered why the marriage never seemed to surface more than a series of arrangements, accommodations, and mutual tolerance.

The bills were split 50/50. Our lives had been structured to be significantly separate. I think there was never a marriage that was more "OPEN" and the estrangement grew. He handed me a book on "Open Marriage" after we got engaged. Guess I should have read it, huh??

After three years I insisted on marriage counseling. The counselor began to encourage that he come. Finally one day he did. I sat there while he told the counselor that I was a bit slow to catch on to things…just not that successful. He explained that no truly ambitious person would have left a prestigious graduate program as I had. He explained that he had to leave me written notes because he was never sure if I comprehended his verbal requests. He felt it difficult to spend "fun time" with me because I was culturally deprived although he recognized that I had potential. I lacked "structure".

He said that he had no problems with the marriage. I had the problems. He explained that counselors were for people with problems and since he felt he had few, if any, he was leaving. The counselor suggested that I leave with him and return next week alone.

I had not wanted to admit that I was more of a convenience than a companion; but the counselor assured me when I returned the next week that this "poor guy" who "needed" me was a classic Type A personality who focused upon my utilitarian value. I was a tool and tools are used to build things. He was building. He was building his future…whether I would have any role in it was quite another matter.

It took awhile. I shed an ocean of tears. I knew there was no point in talking to him. Finally when I felt I had no choice, I announced that this marriage had failed. That it needed to end…for my sake. Somehow and I don't remember how or who, but one of us suggested that perhaps starting a family would help. "Babies bring people closer together, right? The condoms disappeared. I've never taken a birth control pill in my life.

Pregnant yet thinking nothing different about "us" as my third trimester began he announced that he had applied for and been accepted for a 2 month rotation at Columbia University in New York. Pregnancy or no pregnancy this was an opportunity no committed medical student could or would afford to miss…and then he was gone.

I guess I had intuitively expected that despite our two careers, I would shoulder most responsibility for the care of the children, but I had also hoped or dreamed of more than a "Disneyland Dad". My best friend nearly moved in with me. Carrying groceries to the third floor walk up, helping to massage away charley horse cramps in the middle of the night, shopping for baby clothes—these experiences she shared with me to help me get through it all. One day he was back.

He swore that he had taken Lamaze classes while he was out of town and that he wanted to be there when the baby was born. The baby was born.... and indeed he was there. During the separation I had accepted that the baby and I were on our own.

I was barely up off from that awfully cold medical birthing table; barely leaving maternity and entering post-partum when he said: "While you are here why not get your tubes tied?" I thought it was a joke. My first thought was NOBODY is going back in there to do anything!

The next morning my room was filled with Azaleas. The nurses were grinning ear to ear when he appeared.

I don't always respond as I should when I should or could, so two days later I was still thinking. Was that a plea for freedom to love me without more interference? How could someone who would soon have so much not want to share it all with a generation in the making?

We had more potential than most dream of and when courting and we talked of children I told him I planned to have a baseball team…nine children, and his response was "that will be no problem. I will be able to afford it."

When I began to think instead that he might not want me or a family I announced my plans to leave. I remember the dramatic scene six weeks later when I packed our things and announced that we were leaving. He grabbed for my arms and for the baby. We struggled. He said, "No, I plan to keep this family together". I stayed.

Chapter Four: Checkmate

Here we go again. Let's do what we can do with what we have. I had been ready to walk away. Done! Forget it! I'm outta here....but after all the madness with the slightest evidence of caring just a little bit I dug in my heels again.

I was a Doctoral student in Political Science at Tufts and Doctoral Fellow at The Program for Science and International Affairs (PSIA) at Harvard. With the fellowship I got an office, a stipend, access to all resources at both universities, and a secretarial pool. Living in Brookline and shuttling between Medford and Cambridge, somehow I was able to continue plodding along towards my path to specialize in international security and affairs.

He had told me that he was in a five year program, for a M.D.-Ph.D., and it was just so hectic that he needed help typing his research paper. So I took care of the baby, worked on my dissertation and Teaching Assistantship at Tufts, finished my Ford Foundation and Doctoral Fellowships at Harvard, AND typed his darn research paper. I primarily used the secretarial pool to get my papers typed and usually while he was "on call" all night after the baby went to bed I was up typing his research papers.

"Match Day", the day that senior year medical students discover what hospitals they have been matched with was near and I couldn't wait to see if we were moving to D.C., New York City, or staying in Massachusetts since he swore that we would stay on the East Coast so I could develop my contacts on Capitol Hill, Johns Hopkins and Harvard to further develop as a specialist in international affairs.

Mommy and daughter were dressed in matching outfits and as I stood there in that Hall at Harvard I just knew we were about to turn that corner. I was about to get the affirmation that yes he wanted us to stay a family and for me to get a chance to develop the Post Doctoral contacts that would help me build my career.

He opened his envelope and smiled from ear to ear. He was clear across the room and I kept waiting for him to head my way when suddenly I heard one of his fellow Chicago buddies read his letter and shout University of Chicago, you, too!!!!!

-35-

University of Chicago???!!

I was getting flashbacks to 5 years ago when he had led me to believe he had applied to Johns Hopkins and had not. Now he had led me to believe he had not applied to the University of Chicago and had.

Dr. Alvin Pouissant was smiling and watching the faces of the medical students and when his eyes met mine he walked over to me and said, "Are you Okay?" I thought I was going to pass out, but calmly said: "I think I'm gonna need a drink and some therapy……. and in that order!"

He took me into a private room and after he heard my story about what a surprise this was, with his soft, calm, reassuring Deepak Chopra like modulating voice I remember him saying, "hmmm, sounds like you have some interesting choices to make"…and then we both looked at the baby.

The first day that I returned to my office at Harvard I told my program chair that it looked like I would be moving to the Midwest, leaving the East coast. He was not excited, but said let me see what I can do.

A few months later he called me to tell me that he had a few contacts with The U.S. Department of Energy who had a need for consultants at Argonne National Laboratory, which was affiliated with The University of Chicago.

I became a consultant at Argonne shortly after the move. The work, the pay, the terms were astounding.

Chapter Five: The Dissertation

A few months later he finished medical school. I was packing…again and we moved to his hometown, Chicago.

Three months later a drunk driver sped through a red light and rammed into the passenger side of the car. My right leg lodged inside of a space in the passenger door where the speaker had been. The door had actually caved in since mine was the side of the impact.

I had passed out. When I awoke I saw him standing in front of the car…in a mist (or was it steam?) and I just knew this is it. This entire thing has finally wiped me out. The baby and I are dead.

It took awhile for us to get out of the car. An ambulance arrived, but because they were obligated to take us to Jackson Park Hospital he sent them away. He said: "We are going to The University of Chicago and nowhere else!" What?!!!

A stranger who had seen the accident and us walking away, offered to drive us to the hospital of his choice. My collarbone was dislocated and the baby had to receive thirty stitches. Glass had shattered and cut her in so many places. She and I were drenched in blood, mostly resultant from the tiny splinters of glass that had grazed us in several places.

It was a hit and run by an uninsured drunk driver. Everyone begged us to sue but we didn't. I think I'll take the lion's share for that move, arguing as I did that that's why we have a litigious society. Everybody sues. Twenty-five years later I'm still smarting from that one...My collarbone still warns me when it is going to rain.

The toddler and I crawled on the floor for months since it was just too painful to climb in bed or lift her in any way.

That aside there was always the matter of finishing the dissertation. As soon as I was able I went back to my notes and to writing it. Finally months later it was finished. Just keeping it all together had been a chore and the day it was ready I had asked him to pick the completely typed dissertation and original notes up from the typist since he worked two blocks from her.

I don't know what time he came in but when I woke up about 2 a.m. I found him asleep in the bed with our toddler and me. I was sure he was tired so I didn't attempt to wake him. I just started to look for the dissertation. I looked in the family room, the dining room, on the kitchen table, in the bathroom, Everywhere…but nothing. I went out to the car thinking it might be in the trunk or on the backseat. Inside the car, in the trunk, under the hood, and under the car, I couldn't find it. I started to panic so I returned to our bedroom and frantically asked him where it was!!

He said the last thing he remembered was putting it a briefcase before stopping by Kentucky Fried Chicken on 75th Street on his way home. Sleep deprived he had no idea where it or the briefcase were and rolled over.

Crying hysterically, trying to believe this was not happening, I dressed the baby, jumped in the car and drove to Kentucky Fried Chicken. Of course they were closed. Still crying hysterically I walked around the entire store looking for a briefcase on a table or on the floor or on the counter. Anywhere! Then I thought they probably just threw it in the dumpster at the end of the night so I checked on the baby who was asleep in the car and I climbed up the cyclone fence near the dumpster and jumped in. I was thrashing through the trash when a police car pulled up. Two Chicago Policemen screamed, "Hey lady, what do you think you are doing!"

I screamed my story as I held onto the edge of the inside of the dumpster and then they looked at each other and jumped in with me. The three of us went through the trash until they said, "baby I am sorry to tell you but there is no briefcase in here."

They pulled me out, wished me luck and escorted me home. I put the baby in the crib, sat on the side of the bed and stared at him. I've proctored, done his work shifts, typed his research, done pregnancy & parenting nearly by myself, moved repeatedly, dealt with lies, deceit, total disregard for me, and overcome, and laughed and cried throughout this insanity but now this is the night I go to jail!

Hours later I was still awake and then I thought if I murder him, then what? Then everything will have been for nothing. Then what happens to my daughter? By dawn I was accepting that it was simply gone.

It simply vanished; all three hundred pages. The entire dissertation from my original research on "Brazilian Nuclear Development" was just gone.

These were the days of word processors and the typist had surrendered ALL. The only thing I had was shoeboxes of note cards and notebooks from my field research in Brazil and index cards with footnotes that contained the facts and the drafts of chapters that had been edited and refined long ago.

Those who were closest to me kept repeating the same response to my tragedy. "Write it over." In particular, when I called my mom she empathized and in the final analysis asked me: "Who wrote it the first time?? If you wrote it the first time you are the best person to rewrite it!"

I don't know how it was possible, but when confronted with the notion that this was my final defeat, I somehow did just that. Using my notecards and other references I rewrote it. Six weeks later it was rewritten.

Reservations were made and the day he was to drive us to the airport he couldn't get away from the hospital. Luckily his father was home and drove us instead. Pregnant with my second child, I boarded the plane bound for Massachusetts with my toddler and a suitcase full of papers. My committee had been totally supportive throughout the ordeal.

My best friend (who nearly lived with me throughout his absence during the last trimester of the first pregnancy), allowed me and my toddler to stay with her while I prepared for my oral examination.

I typed the final chapter, photocopied the final sections, entered the examination room and to my own surprise…PASSED!! Despite it all and with the help of many, including a faculty advocate, I had done it!!

I was allowed to march in commencement the following year and you know who flew into Boston as a surprise to hand me a dozen roses as I left the stage with my degree. My mom was the only other person who came. Four months before the graduation I had a second child, a son. My mom sat in the audience with our 3 year old daughter and 4

month old son and she and I were just speechless.
Nonetheless; mission accomplished!

Chapter Six: The Concession

I returned to Chicago determined to take my new degree and two children wherever I could go. One day while sitting on the bed I decided to challenge Buddhism. I had gone to meetings, read the brochures, chanted a little, but I needed what they called "actual proof"...not some theoretical "stuff" but a miracle. I decided to search for a house.

His parents owned the six flat we lived in so our apartment was only $150 a month and while that was a bargain it seemed impossible to get rid of the roaches and mice that were a constant problem.

One night I heard my son cry out from his crib and when I saw a mouse run down the side of the bars I said, "that's it"....with him or without him we are getting out of here.

I got a HUD list and other general real estate publications and every day I would hunt for a house. I told everyone we knew to let me know if they found the miracle house. We did not have the money for a down payment on a house but I got the conviction that there was a house in Chicago that belonged to me!

He was completely nonchalant about the entire endeavor. What a joke! On our salaries and with our debt?? He was sure that nothing would come of it. Months and months of looking at auctions and boarded up properties and sheriff and tax lien sales and just about nothing on the "open" market since I, too, thought that a bit beyond my reach. So I just kept chanting.

One day I got a call from his Aunt who said, "I just found your house". It was a Prairie Style home designed by a student of Frank Lloyd Wright, Charles E. White. Four bedrooms, a full and half bath, a full basement, lots of land for flowers, swing sets, backyard parties, an attic, 2,000 sq. feet, spacious first floor and asking price $79,500.

I ran to the newsstand and bought the paper where she said the description was listed. I called the owners who JUST happened to be home. They said, "You can come right now if you would like to see it." I jumped in the car, rushed right over there. I was instantly amazed and in love with it. I picked up the phone and called him to tell him I was in our new house. Then a second mystical thing happened. He was between commitments and had time to run over to the house, which he did. Within two hours of his Aunt's call he AND I had seen the house and we were saying "We will take it."

Between the credit checks, the first contract to buy, the contract reviews by lawyers, my chanting on the miracle, our work obligations, and juggling it all a "you won't believe it" happened. Not only did we not have any money in the bank or collateral, but suddenly the down payment appeared.

His mother who was totally in favor of us getting the house suddenly inherited what we needed for a down payment and within a month we were the new owners, the new family on the block, living in a house.

I think considering the lost dissertation, all that had gone on and where we were headed, the house was a concession…and a nice one at that and I got my first conspicuous big benefit, actual proof, from chanting!

Chapter Seven: Valentine's Day

We moved in the house the Fall following my
march across that stage. He was nearing the
midpoint of his Residency and I was teaching. I was
beginning to learn about community organizing and,
in fact, was recruited at a local block club meeting
to become Executive Director of an organization
sponsored by the local Chamber of Commerce to
facilitate revitalization of 71st Street commercial
strip in cooperation with The Chicago Department
of Economic Development and South Shore Bank.

The job required civic engagement, outreach
to community residents, business owners, non-profit
organizations, elected and appointed officials. I
began to develop quite a few networks and
affiliations and funding to implement a façade
rebate program for 71st Street businesses.

We seemed to be settling into some routine
that involved my community outreach and the
completion of the medical training years. He
thought my outreach would be very helpful when he
launched his practice and I was beginning to find a

way to use my skills, juggle personal roles, and find some sense of fulfillment.

I thought great time to have another baby. He wasn't thrilled but agreed. He said: "We already have the perfect pair, a boy and a girl" I replied: "Yeah, but we will need a tie breaker!" I thought we're making compromises. We are both getting what we need. Things must be better.

Valentine's Day was approaching and he said about a month in advance, "So since I can set aside either the day or the evening for us to do something together, which would you prefer?

Our neighbor down the street had to told me she was planning a "Lover's Brunch" for couples around noon so I said, "how about the day?"

Her home was decorated for lovers with cupids and roses and love music and tons of food and good conversation. We started actually having an incredibly good time together so I whispered in his ear, "and now I want the whole day." He must have been feeling the same because he said, "Ok, let me make a phone call."

I thought he probably had to get another doctor to take over a hospital shift, but then the wife came back from the kitchen and whispered in my ear that he was on the phone and had said, "I'm sorry, but I am going to have to break our date and I hope I can have a rain check."

About an hour later we left and he drove straight to a Supper Club called The Park West. The valet took the car and when we got to the door he pulled out two tickets for the Angie Bofill concert. The hostess said there were no seats in the front but could sit us in the middle of the audience. He pulled out a $50 and all of a sudden seats appeared in the second row.

After the third song I leaned over and said, "So who were you bringing to the Angie Bofill concert after you took me home from the brunch?" He said, "What difference does it make? You're here aren't you?"

Our second daughter and third child was born the next month.

Chapter Eight: Until Death Do Us Part

I am not sure how or why, but we lasted another year. A house, a new baby, and a maid later we continued to coexist. The specter of dissolution (a final ending) was a constant daunting reality of daily life. It was almost like always waiting for the other shoe to drop.

We had gone from the days when he never came home because of his medical training to the ones when he never came home because of his moonlighting.....or whatever!

Then one day out of the blue he drove up in his new car, a bronze Toranado with a phone inside. He was alarmingly agreeable and friendly and then he asked me to train myself through the American Medical Association so I could organize his medical practice. If I would agree to put his practice together, using my contacts (as a professor, community organizer and leadership in various organizations) and skills then the financial arrangements for our roles would be carefully defined.

Things would be official and detached. In fact, an accountant had advised him that writing off my services would just about offset what financially supporting the children and me was costing him. He not only proposed it but he put his proposal in writing.

I argued that this "employer-employee" arrangement would serve as little more than a prelude to divorce. He admitted after much discussion that he wanted to be married AND he wanted his freedom-emotionally and even financially. He was tired of paying babysitters and nursery schools and for anything but the things he wanted and needed. The original formulas for a 50/50 split had been altered by the fact that he now earned much more than I did as a university lecturer and with a home and children our costs had gone up...not to mention student loans and other debts accrued along the way.

I gambled that he was less sure about what he wanted than he thought. Perhaps he was just being dramatic so I enrolled in the AMA course to set up the files and the practice and to launch the practice for him. I was wrong. He knew what he was doing. He was preparing his "getaway".

I spent the next quarter working with the widow who gave (not sold) him her husband's practice. The practice had been lucrative and stable for over thirty years. Her spouse had died suddenly and left her wanting to find someone to carry on his good works. My husband had heard of this man's death and had offered to buy the practice. When the widow met our three children, all under the age of five, she was deeply touched and refused to accept any price for the practice.

Instead, she offered to help him launch his new practice by writing her personal letter to patients urging them to accept this new physician as the heir to her husband's practice.

After I took the 3 and 5 year old to nursery school, Monday through Friday, the widow and I met for months...going over patient files, coordinating the mailings about the succession, planning the opening reception, etc. So many times I wanted to ask her if what I was doing was wrong, foolish.... sick. I wanted to ask if her marriage to a physician had been worth the experience. I wanted to ask her if she would have chosen a life with her own mate if she had known how it would unfold.

I wanted to ask her if her creature comforts had been worth the trade-offs. The big house, the luxury cars and trips and perks....Had they been in love and had that love lasted? Were her children happy and did they benefit from such a marriage?

There were so many things that I wanted to ask. I never got the courage to ask even one of my questions. Instead I would look into her eyes and at her hands for the clues and answers I was seeking, but we continued to be formal with one another. I had not been honest, had she? We never spoke of personal things. She often cried throughout our work. Her grief seemed always there. I never wanted to add confusion to her misery so I kept my thoughts and own tears to myself. There I was presenting myself as a dutiful wife when, in fact, I was just working on a contract. Our relationship had just become a deal.

He continued to be "on call". Then one day he asked if we could "talk". The "talk" was his announcement that he had rented an apartment.

Maybe neither of us knew what to do about how we were feeling. The talk started with him saying that he had been required by one of his suburban hospitals to prove he resided within ten minutes of the job. He started to explain that for this reason the apartment was little more than a technicality…just something he had to do to keep this extra source of income.

As my silence grew deafening, he confessed he was feeling cramped and confined…that he had missed most of the fun of life due his many years in school and that at a time when his years of training were finally coming to an end he felt he should be allowed to have what he wanted when he wanted it and how he wanted it.

He felt a longing for something he could not define. In part, he sensed that what he sought could be found outside the confines of what he had. He announced his intentions to "sow wild oats", to be "free" to take a leave of absence from responsibilities.

He had asked me the last several years of our time together what I thought about "swinging". Our conversations about that went something like:

"What would you think about swinging"

"Swinging from what?"

" No, partner swapping."

"You mean like sleeping with other people while you watch and vice-versa??"

" Yep, something like that."

" Soooo we would do foursomes then get up and have coffee, eggs and bacon, carry on our lives as if nothing happened?"

" Yep, something like that."

" How about a "hell to tha no!"

He bought some incredibly sexy outfits for me to wear to events and then he would watch men and women watching me. Before the night was over he would say "if you were going to sleep with somebody here who would it be?" Yeah, I think I should have read that book on "Open Marriage".

Nearly one month after the practice was nearly ready and our second mortgage for $50,000 approved, I noticed that item-by-item, his desk, files and other work-related materials disappeared from the home. When I asked about this he told me he was just taking the "basics" to the apartment he had rented.

The closer he came to completing his nine years of training, the more his belongings left the house.

Five months before he left for the last time certified mail from a female started coming to the home. He told me that she was a neurotic female who was seeking verification of his home address to prevent him from being accepted to staff at a suburban hospital. I dropped the inquisition and did as he had asked to just never sign for the letters.

I guess we both could feel the end was near. Filled with mixed emotions about it, I could feel myself coming unglued. I wouldn't "swing". As much as I tried, the "trophy wife" thing was more than incredibly boring. The constant travel to medical conferences and leaving the kids behind was increasingly uncomfortable and taking them with us was definitely a drag for him. It just wasn't working.

Three weeks before he left we went to dinner and drinks at a Piano Bar. I took a valium that he had prescribed for me and a drink and the next thing I knew I was again at home.

I heard that after I got to the club I had decided to join the pianist and sing "God Bless The Child That's Got His Own" until security hauled me away. The next thing that I remembered was waking up on the stairs in my home smelling of liquor and urine. Evidently after I passed out I peed on myself.

As I cried and crawled upstairs to our bed I could hear my heart pounding and I knew I was finally coming completely unglued. I couldn't "not react" anymore and I couldn't "fix it". When I made it to the bed I woke him up and begged him to take me somewhere...to see someone who could help me.

Rehab. A psychiatrist. Anybody, anytime, Anywhere.

Was he disconnected, disaffected, or just disinterested? I'll never know. That night there was no response and I just finally fell asleep.

Two days later he dressed for work and as he headed for the door he said, "I'm leaving and am never coming back. You're pathetic."

Chapter Nine: The Jedi's

After several days of feeling tremendous relief, the mudslide began.

Nothing was fine.

For a week I spoke to no one about "it". Finally week two I sobered up long enough to panic and I started telling my story.

Men, married and single, were at my door everyday with a bottle and a shoulder to cry on. Women, their wives, or acquaintances called to hear the gory details and never ended a conversation without offering to call him "to talk some sense into him".

He called me one day and asked me to please stop giving out his number. Those that had not called him to preach had called him to date. None of them knew or cared about his debts or mine. To the needy and the greedy he was just young, available and quite employed.

The week that the cupboard became bare I went to the bank to withdraw some funds and was directed to customer service where I was informed by a sympathetic bank Vice-President that all funds had been withdrawn from that account before it was closed. There was no money.... at least for me.

The bank customer service representative said, "baby, we all wondered why you didn't set up a joint account for the mortgage money once it was transferred to checking."

I couldn't think of an answer or think period and the next thing I knew I was walking down the street.

That was the same day one of the doctor's wives who I knew called to ask me where I was and who was the woman with him in Dallas (at a conference for physicians) who was pretending to be me.

It was also the same day the pre-school called about the late tuition bill, when I first tried to get food stamps, and discovered (that based upon his income since we were still married), I didn't qualify, and the first time I had to "borrow" food.

He didn't just leave. He took all the money with him. It wasn't long before my car was nearing repossession, the home foreclosure, my credit cards in default, home phone, alarm and utilities disconnected and car, medical, and life insurance cancelled.

Understanding creditors ceased to understand. His creditors were hounding me every day since he would not respond to them. The emergency food programs, generous neighbors, churches, and friends were the only reason we were eating and even that was being done on a camper's stove, and homework being done by the light of kerosene lamps and candles. Thank goodness for having been a Den Mother!

During our "utilitilessness" I discovered how important routine was for children. When the phone went I made a list of people who lived nearby who agreed to receive messages from my parents who lived in another state. I had not told my parents what was going on, but when the phone was disconnected they knew something drastic had happened.

I found every pay phone in the neighborhood (these days there are none) and often walked the children to one so we could call their grandparents collect. They felt better knowing those other familiar voices were accessible. Talking on the phone became a real treat. When the gas went, I heated water and cooked with the camping equipment.

The children were initially 1, 3, and 5 years old when this "happened". We formed teams so we could help one another get enough hot water for a bath or enough warmth when it was cold. When your lifestyle crashes, a small check doesn't go very far. It took this Ph.D. three months to face reality and another six months to find a job.

I remember the night I returned home to find that when I flipped the switch nothing happened. We came in the house, stumbled up the stairs, and after I lit two candles everybody sat right up under me. Their eyes were as big as saucers and they seemed to be in utter shock and I thought okay, you'd better think quick so I said, "Okay, well I guess it's finally time to tell you that when you are 1, 3, and 5 that special children are selected to go through what is called "Jedi Training!" "Jedi Training!? What is that?" they shouted.

"Tell us, what is Jedi Training? I marvel now at my spontaneous creativity when I said, "Jedi Training is a testing period to see if today's children can become tomorrow's leaders by surviving several months without any support from the major system. If you can use your mind and all of the creativity that is within you to survive without the luxuries of modern society, then you will truly be Jediis!"

Then I told them stories of Daniel Boone fighting to survive in the wilderness when there was no electricity or telephone or gas. We talked about the Jedi warriors of the sci-fi world and how they demonstrated their powers to survive. I talked and they listened…and listened…and listened. I think all of us were especially tired that day and after burning three long candles, we fell asleep together on the carpet on the living room floor.

The next day I found an Army/Navy store where I bought hats, flashlights, armbands, and bicycle shop miscellaneous "Jedi" materials. I stopped at a bicycle shop to buy fluorescent strips like the ones that go on the bikes to alert drivers of night bicyclers. I found emergency flares and fluorescent light sticks in the basement. On my lunch break one day, I placed fluorescent strips on the floor to mark a path for walking. I carefully placed the flashlights, hats and supplies directly inside the front door where I also kept a volume of the encyclopedia that contained nursery rhymes, songs and stories so we could sing camping songs, while "camping" inside.

I remember the first day that to their surprise Jedi materials were at the house awaiting their return at the end of the day. When we entered the house, I said, "Look! Your first supplies for Jedi training have been left here by the Master Jedi's." "Wow!" they said, "What do we do?" Tell us again what is Jedi Training?!"

At this point Jedi training could be whatever I designed it to be so I repeated, "Jedi training is a testing period to see if today's children can become tomorrow's leaders by surviving several months without any support from the major system. If you can use your mind and all of the creativity that is

within you to survive without the luxuries of
modern society, then you will truly be Jedi's!"

Everyday as they prepared for school, they
would splash in cold water and say with a sparkle,
"just like Daniel Boone!" I didn't know how long
the utilities would be off so I gradually made the
Jedi game more interesting. Every night when we
returned home they would put on their hats and arm
bands. In the dark the light from the flashlights
reflected off the strips and they were able to follow
markers to get through the house without stumbling.

It was like having your own cave…only this
cave was a house.

They would giggle as they put on their hats and
armbands and carried their flashlights. We entered
the house and on the bricks in front of the fireplace
there was the camping stove. I would prepare hot
dogs.

They would sit there and concentrate with total
sincerity. They had a new reality; a new ritual.
They had seen enough to believe this Jedi training
thing was real.

Could there be real Jedi's? Could they become Jedi's? Would they successfully complete the training and how would they know when that would be? Had this series of unexpected events been leading to this exciting training?

Throughout the month since their dad had left, everything had seemed to fall apart, but could the turn of events have been leading to a new dawn? Their faces glowed and they wanted so badly to ask their friends at school if they too had been through Jedi training, but to ask such a thing was not something Jedi's in training could do. (This instruction was to keep The Department of Children & Family Services at bay.) They contained their anticipation and excitement and we bonded as a foursome who could transcend and succeed.

The Jedi fantasy lessened the trauma, as it would with any children in similar circumstances. I was learning the value of creativity in coping with the catastrophe we were in.

"It's not what happens to you but how you respond to what is happening to you that makes all the difference!"

Chapter Ten: The "D" Word

He left just before Halloween. Shortly after
Thanksgivings I received a letter from a lawyer
advising me of her plans to petition for dissolution
of marriage at his request. Nothing materialized
after this letter but within sixty days of that scare I
acted to protect us by going to a lawyer myself.

His Aunt had been married to a lawyer and
recommended a lawyer to me took who mercy on
my plight and as a "professional courtesy" for the
Aunt who made the referral, she required no
payment upfront.

She was awesome, firm, commanding,
demanding, precise, experienced and prepared to get
results. She filed papers in February and the process
was on. Another major thing had happened. I had
decided to consistently and seriously chant.

I had first encountered Nichiren Buddhism in
1971 while in Brazil as an exchange student. Then
in 1978 shortly after the move to Chicago I had met
another Buddhist, who frequently invited me to

meetings, taught me how to chant and told me what practicing Buddhism could mean to my life.

He had disapproved of "chanting" but he was gone and I needed a miracle! He had taken all of the money out of the bank, moved in with a woman, skipped providing for our welfare, and what if he moved out of state? What if he changed his identity? What if he never paid the mortgage or caught up on costs for the children? Each month we were further and further behind. Just a month earlier I had written out checks to pay the bills and when I got to ten thousand dollars, the stack of bills was still tall..so you can imagine how quickly and how hard you can fall four months after no longer having the money to cover that lifestyle.

I remember when I had called my Buddhist friend to announce that he had left us. She knew that his disapproval of me chanting had been my major obstacle to embracing the practice so her first response was, "Great, now you can really practice!"

That was not exactly the response I was expecting so I had hung up on her. Yet that December just a few days after his 32nd birthday and a few days before mine I joined. Like Tina Turner,

Herbie Hancock, Patrick Duffy, Wayne Shorter, Orlando Bloom, and others I became a Buddhist, chanting Nam-Myoho-Renge-Kyo (devotion to the mystic law of cause and effect through sound or original teaching).

I went from always crying and drinking and dreading the avalanche of sudden and immediate needs that life required when you are trying to feed, educate, and raise three children with no money, to chanting with them to "fix" it. Was this like that Jedi training? Was this a way to transcend this? If so the children were on board 100% and so was I.

I also joined a small eight member support group facilitated by a psychologist and sponsored by a major non-profit just to get myself ready to say the "D" word and then to file for it.

I don't care what anybody tells you about his or her divorce, yours is as unique as your shoe size and the options available require research, and commitment. It's no simple process when there are property and custody issues.

Here I was about to join the "First Wives Club"…now the meaning of that was starting to hit home. Like seasons that change, people change and the long, demanding, draining, struggling years of medical training could change both people and seasons.

I landed a job seven months after he left. He had caught up on the mortgage but had only given me $150 a month so I had lived off the loans and gifts from my parents, family, and friends. The job enabled me to get the utilities back on and the lawyer deposed him and got court orders forcing him to "catch up" on spousal and child support.

The more pressure he got to get current on that the more he called and connected. There were many times when he had called to arrange visitation with the children but just didn't show. Sometimes he would call to say he wouldn't be coming and sometimes he just didn't show.

It could have been the nature of his work with medical emergencies. He no doubt had a mudslide of his own. The euphoria did not last long nor did the fifty thousand dollars we borrowed on the house and that he took out of the bank. Then one day he called to ask if he could come by to see them at the house rather than taking them out.

-71-

I went upstairs and went to bed, leaving them private time alone and when I awoke around 2 a.m. the children were in bed and he was asleep on the couch. That was the last time he ever spent a night with all of us.

I think he was trying the home on to see if it fit anymore. Maybe he was feeling at a crossroads. Maybe he was homesick. About eight months into the divorce process he called and asked if we could talk. He came by and said he was trying to think about how we could put this all behind us and reconcile.

He had enjoyed the company of lots of different women, many of whom he even brought with him when he picked up the children. He said things had not really worked out as he had hoped and I knew the lawyer was applying serious pressure in all directions. He said it was his opinion that he should just come home.

I called everyone excited. "He says he is coming home!" He never came. In fact, after that discussion he grew bitter and did not visit the children for several months.

With my tax refund I paid to participate in the Buddhist Pilgrimage to Japan where I could chant on sacred temple grounds and with the High Priests to have it all end best for us all.

When I returned, the divorce sped up. I rolled up my Gohonzon (our scroll, object of workship) and drove to the Buddhist Chicago Cultural Center. A married couple was responsible for all organizational activities at that time. The wife had become a friend who had chanted with me for days and weeks and months. I told her my story and its final result. "I chanted for him to come home. I even spent my entire tax refund to go to Japan to visit the head temple grounds to make this happen and now the divorce has sped up! This doesn't work and you can have it back!" She responded calmly and said that of course she would happily accept it if I was prepared to be so shallow as to think it was a magic wand when the magic and the wand were inside of me. Did I want to turn myself in as well?

If this result was indeed the final chapter of my entire life then she would accept my surrender. If I did not have the courage or the wisdom to continue facing my own karma no matter the details of disappointments then she would understand. BUT if I was prepared ignore temporary results for greater, more profound, and lasting ones then she suggested we return to my home, re-enshrine the Gohonzon and celebrate the turn of events as the details of another day rather than the sentence of a life-time.

Relative happiness and absolute happiness were oceans apart. If arrogance and anger could persuade me so easily to ignore the mission ahead then I might miss the opportunities that were on the other side of transforming my life rather than acquiescing to it. Olympians suffer small setbacks yet win gold medals because of invoking the discipline to fight until the race was won rather than when just having one day of a great practice.

Without faith there could be no Buddhism and without Buddhism there could be no fundamental transformation. Which did I prefer, immediate results or lasting ones? Even if he did come back would I have been a great wife, mother and person or he a great father, husband, person without chanting?

I think we got to my house, re-enshrined the Gohonzon, did the evening prayers, and chanted thirty minutes just in time for me to go pick up the children.

Chapter Eleven: Post Decree

The divorce was granted twenty-nine months after my petition and granted on the grounds of mental cruelty. The one thing he had never challenged was custody. His issues had all related to money. I asked for him to pay the mortgage and child support. Throughout the ordeal I had two lawyers. Both were excellent and thorough.

The first lawyer quit my case and sued me when I had refused to audit his practice, pursue alimony, pension, and life insurance and other terms that would have protected and provided for us. She had argued that I was due a more reasonable settlement and while she was technically correct since I had "been there" throughout nine years of the medical training I had different concerns.

In addition, as I had quit my job at his request to put his practice together she wanted me to seek compensation for that. We had a maid who cared for the youngest child and the house and the two older children attended private Montessori school. She argued (justifiably) that my/our lifestyle should not be compromised by the end of the marriage.

While I felt that the children were entitled to financial support from us both for their education, lessons, clothing, travel, food, medical care, grooming, and general welfare I felt uncomfortable with the notion of extracting money for myself. I had this moral dilemma.

I viewed the issue of alimony as a romantic, not a pragmatist. How could this love and support that had been given so freely now be defined by cash value? As if a dollar value per year could now be assessed like one would do for a condo? If there were children then it was they would should be cared for by both parents; but adults (I felt) were on their own.

Besides without constantly seeking court sanctions there was no way to guarantee that court ordered alimony would ever be sent and alimony was considered taxable income. Lawyers warned also that without continually going to court there were never any guarantees that one would receive alimony. Although I never asked for it or received it I was still audited by the IRS for years and years as he claimed alimony payments to me on his taxes. While I probably did a lot to live up to my noble and romantic values, I did little to actually spare myself alimony-related grief.

I felt that I had earned a Ph.D. and would earn a living. I agreed to full custody and that he pay the mortgage to provide for their housing. I deleted any request for him covering anything else other than child support and mortgage payments. I accepted full responsibility for marital debts that I had created and asked only that he provide for his children.

By the time that the divorce was decreed the distance between us was well established; yet I remember wondering how would it change me. This thing of being ..."divorced".

I spent hours that morning trying to dress...and remembering asking myself what was appropriate to wear to one's divorce. According to traditions and rituals, certain colors are appropriate for certain events.

You wear white for weddings, cotillions, and debutante balls.... Black for funerals, those in grief, pink for girls, blue for boys. But what do you wear to your divorce? Do you dress up? Do you dress down? Do you dress professional? Do you dress dowdy? Do you dress or should you be "dressed" happy or do you dress "sad"?

I couldn't sleep the night before. The hours of staring at the ceiling had led to the creation of scenarios and expectations for this ritual about to happen. No matter what I had expected, nothing could have prepared me for what actually occurred.

Nothing.

It was all so matter-of-fact. The lawyers said this. The lawyers said that. I spoke under oath. The mallet fell and swish, it was all over. I walked outside the courtroom into the hall and nobody seemed to know, notice, or care that there I was, the un-Mrs. I passed them in the hall, elevators, on the streets and through the lot of cars. I drove away and it seemed that no one even gave a damn…because they didn't. It was only a day that changed my life…not that of others.

Just that quickly all of the years, the compromises, the negotiations, and the dreams vanished. I had no parties. I made no calls, except to my parents and all I said was, "It's over". They sighed with relief because it had been a great emotional and financial strain on them and they said, "thank goodness, now you can get on with your life"...and what did that mean? Wasn't all of this a part of my life, too?

When it started they were 1, 3, and 5. I walked into that courtroom a married woman and left there a single female and head of household with three children ages, 5, 7, and 9.

The hearing was early in the day and I was home a little after lunch. I came home and sat on the back porch steps staring out at the yard.

The sky was blue. The grass was green. The lilies were in bloom and the weather was not too warm. I reviewed it all and thought I don't know if I want to even try and imagine what's next. The dating had started in 1972 and the wedding was in 1974. The children were born in 1977, 1980, and 1982. The dissertation had disappeared and was written in 1979. The medical training had ended in June of 1983 and the separation began that October and now, on July 9, 1986 the divorce was official.

After nearly three years of depositions, interrogatories, continuances, legal research and court appearances, it was finally over. My portion of legal fees for the divorce had cost $12,000 and he was responsible for all of that. The property was quit claim deeded to me with it being his obligation to pay along with child support. Lawyers get paid!

I didn't take any portion of pensions, nor alimony, nor health or life insurance benefits and I assumed responsibility for my own credit card debts and could look forward to repaying my parents for chunks of legal fees they had paid.

I couldn't help but recall the pledges throughout the years that even if we were getting in debt to pay for our careers, we needn't worry because he would ultimately earn the money necessary to pay for everything.

While I once was a person who frowned on bankruptcy, I now judged no one for filing it. Late payments, slow payments, no payments; somehow in time everyone had to be paid, especially my parents who insisted that I needed to take responsibility for the indebtedness I had co-created.

I will never know if theirs was an ethical position, but they emphasized that since I had enjoyed the use of everything we were indebted for that I should pay debtors whether he ever did or not.

By the time of the divorce I had been working two months and my first month on salary I had already been garnished for a lease on a medical office he had refused to pay.

I sat on those steps thinking that, well at the very least this next chapter should be interesting.

That's when he appeared.

Chapter Twelve: The Wizard

He had probably knocked or rung the bell but I hadn't heard it so he had walked around to the back and the first thing he said, was "So how is the good doctor doing?"

This was the handy man that worked for the neighbor directly behind my house. He had cut my grass, fixed a plumbing problem, and generally did odd jobs on the block.

He said he was coming by to check on me and to see if there was any work he could do. Then he repeated, "How is the doctor? I told him the doctor was gone and that our divorce was just final hours ago. He looked me squarely in the eye and said: "Well, I am talking to the doctor." We both smiled. I told him I had work but no money, three small children, a job that didn't pay much and no clue of how I would juggle the tasks ahead.

He said, "Well why don't you let me help until you get on your feet. I'm pretty good around the house and am a pretty good cook." He said he had just had a fire in his home and it was going to be quite awhile before he could live in it again. It would be a blessing for us both if he could move into the basement, be around to help with the children, the cooking, the cleaning, the yard and the property maintenance.

Like a Man Friday…like a Valet? The idea seemed wild, bizarre, and yet I immediately said I would give it a try if he would.

For the next two years he was there to drive me to work, them to school, meetings, programs, lessons, activities. He cooked. He cleaned. He shopped. He chopped (wood for the fireplace). The house was clean. The laundry was done. The beds were made and by the time he came to round us all up at the end of the day dinner was already on the stove. If I had to work late or on the weekends, he kept them entertained until it was time to pick me up.

By day I worked at refining strategies to coordinate lobbying initiatives for the various departments and providing assistance on position papers presented by my agency. Any spare time I could get on weekends and week days were spent building contracts for a consulting firm I formed.

He took care of everything I had no experience with or inclination to do. More than the things he did, he had mother wit and common sense and street sense. He was like a grandfather, father, butler, child care provider and so many things rolled into one person.

He was not formally educated, but he was an educator. He taught the children to respect me.... even when I could not respect myself. He taught them to make every effort everyday to do something nice for one another and for me. He never laid a hand on any of us—except perhaps to shake someone's hands. He drove us all over the country whenever someone paid for me to speak, or consult, or train. One year I was sent (all expenses paid) to speak in thirteen states and we drove to nearly each one. While I worked he took the children to see the sights in cities we visited.

It was his suggestion that I always request travel and lodging accommodations for my driver and family. While other trainers left their children behind, mine were always a stone's throw away.

-85-

They got to meet people from all over the country, ride in limousines, attend luncheons, dinners, special events, and training sessions.

Upon reflection this was a tremendous and marvelous thing because between the legal fees, his salary (room and board included), and general expenses the two years were financially lean but emotionally rich.

Contractors paid for travel, lodging, and meals and my children got to enjoy the rich experiences of my professional life despite our otherwise tight budget. They were greeted warmly by all of the people in the organizations I trained.

The lawyers had been right. I had no idea how demanding and costly it would be to raise three children. It was a never-ending story. I can't find my shoes. I can't reach the shelf (Bang!). I can't do this or that and I'm scared! Please hold me, rock me, sing to me, read to me. Come to my recital. Did you see my work on display at the PTA meeting?

"Friends" would invite the children over to "give me a break" and then interrogate them for hours. "So does your daddy ever spend the night? Does that man who lives with your mommy ever sleep with mommy? Gradually I had to make it just a foursome and the wizard.

I had them in swimming, tennis, piano and violin lessons, scouting, school choirs, recitals, summer camps, and programs. Sports, music and books were priorities in my home. I sat the television on the sidewalk in front of the house and said we would be our own entertainment. We wrote scripts and acted them out. We wrote songs and sang them. We created creative visualization boards and chanted on them.

When the two year contract for my training services ended so did the travel. The pace slowed considerably. Within a few years there were graduations. No longer toddlers they were entering elementary, junior ,and high school. The years of severe trauma had consumed my energies.

Nothing was easy, but without the wizard I wonder how any of so many of the transitional pleasures of life would have been possible.

After dinner and a good night story, the wizard would make me a cocktail and we would talk about my day. What happened, should have happened, didn't happen, could happen....these were matters he discussed with me and in the most humble and generous way he was there to offer suggestions about improving everything.

He had the car to do with as he wished from 9-5 weekdays and most nights after the children were in bed and our nightly chat complete he left for parts unknown and returned in the morning to fix breakfast.

When their dad showed up to pick them up for visitations to spare me the necessity of doing so, he answered to door respectfully, invited him in, called the children down, and off they went.

The wizard respected the father, the mother, the children. It worked. He got paid, had transportation, helped with everything but bringing in the "bacon" and helped us all mend. The entire arrangement was a win-win.

Have you ever had a wizard? Someone who helps you think things through, get things done, stays impartial and when it is time, leaves? Who gets a wizard in their life? Can you requisition one? If you could I guess that everyone would have one. When repairs to his home were complete and it was time to go, he did.

The magician, guru, shaman, griot, who was a shining light, steel and solid pillar, had kept me from sliding deeper into the pit of despair that a wrenching experience like mine can cause. The genie allowed me to nurse my bottle, juggle my chores, roles and responsibilities throughout those two years of transitional hell. My caretaker, nurse, social worker, butler, chauffeur had yanked my coat tails just before I slid too far into an abyss. He had come out of nowhere. This guardian angel had come for me. He had come for them.

Just after he started work for me he would rub the walls and himself with oils and he would say he was going to do all he could to help me, but he had no doubts that the devil was not happy to have him do so. He said, "I don't know who you are or why I am here to save you, but you must be worth it."

It wasn't difficult to appreciate the concept of protection from the Buddhist gods….that the

universe wants to protect us. It was not difficult to
be grateful everyday for this person coming out of
nowhere just in the nick of time.

Chapter Thirteen: Coming Home

Performers from Cirque de Soleil had nothing on me. The crisis after crisis. The running from here to there. The meeting deadlines only to fold into another. Indeed the pace, the demands, the surprises, the innovation to manage it all had tied all four of us in knots. Maybe it was time for "therapy".

I took suggestions from colleagues and associates to find a family therapist to give the four of us a means to talk about what we had been going through. Finally I selected someone who was affordable and highly recommended. During the third session my son giggled after we discussed something about it all that really wasn't funny, but I thought he must be feeling nervous. The therapist walked over to him, asked him to get out of the chair, moved his chair to face a corner and told him to sit in it and then she said, "since you think something is funny, you are now invisible."

Invisible? Invisible? Who would tell a child they were invisible? Before we could resume the "therapy" I told all of the children to get their coats. Then I told her, "Goodbye. If he is invisible then so is my check and my crew. We're outta here." So that was as far as family therapy got.

That night we attended our Buddhist discussion meeting and to my surprise, my oldest daughter stood up and said: "Good evening!" Then she announced her name and said: "I was very sad when my parents got separated and divorced. We did not have money, or food, or lights, or heat but when we started chanting everything turned around. We got food, my mom got a job, our lights and gas came back on. Tonight my mom took us to see a lady who was supposed to be smart who could help us, but she could not then I realized that even smart people need to chant. I am no longer sad because I realize it was my karma to have parents who separated and divorced and if we had not had our problems we would not have chanted so I have decided to chant more!"

She became the first person to get up in the morning to chant and the first person to ask everyday if we could go to a meeting to chant. Without any hesitation she started writing plays and songs about chanting and recruiting everyone in the group to participate. Of course her first recruits were her sister and brother! She found a role for everyone and then she met a young woman who asked if she wanted to come to practices for a cultural festival that young women from all over the country would be performing at in Valley Forge, PA. For the next two months immediately after leaving school we stopped to eat something on the way to the Chicago Buddhist Center so she could practice for the program in Pennsylvania.

If she missed a step she calmly did it over. If she couldn't get a routine she practiced it over and over again until she got it right. If you have ever seen determination, this was it.

About a month into practices I was told by Senior leaders that they did not want to disappoint me but there was NO way she was going to be able to perform with the others in Pennsylvania although they would let her practice. She was too young and the guidelines did not allow for participants her age.

When she got ever more persistent about her practices these leaders advised the teenage group leaders to inform her that she was too young and would never actually be able to attend the convention or perform out of town. She would say okay and then she would tell the others, "when we get to

Pennsylvania we will do this and we will do that"
and I started to wonder if she was losing touch
with reality. Didn't she understand the words that
were coming from the leaders?? If she practiced day
and night she was never going.

I tried to talk to her. Fearing that she would be
crushed if she did not get to go, I tried to explain
that it was wonderful that she wanted to attend the
practices, but I wanted her to completely understand that she wasn't going. The more we all talked
to her to more she chanted and the harder she
practiced and the more she talked about how great
they would be when they performed in Pennsylvania.

I thought, okay I know I lost it a long time ago
and now she's headed for the deep end. What am I
going to do when she is not allowed to go??

The practices continued, the lists of members
going was confirmed, performers were selected,
costumes were fitted, and itineraries were
distributed. Not for one second was she included on
anything. The night before their departure we
attended practice and then there were hugs and
smiles and plans finalized. The bus was leaving at 9
a.m.

I watched her face as we drove home and she looked like a kid who was expecting Santa Claus! She came home and did her chores, smiled, hugged us all and said goodnight. I thought, okay, she is handling this really well.

The phone rang at 6:30 a.m. and it was a call of desperation from one of the Senior Leaders. Suddenly without warning the one person who knew the routine my daughter shadowed had become ill and couldn't go. The group really needed someone who already knew the routine and they needed for her to go. Could she?

I went to wake her up to tell her what had happened. She pulled back the covers and was fully dressed and ready to go. They would be gone overnight and had been told to bring a change of clothes. Her bag was packed.

She never missed a beat. She washed her face and brushed her teeth. We got in the car. We made it there with time to spare so I asked, "but what about the trip fee, and this and that??" The trip had been paid for by the other participant whose parents did not want a refund so there was no new fee required. The costume was even the same size.

When she got on the bus everyone cheered and shouted her name and then it hit me. She never expected NOT to go. She never thought for a second that her dream would not come true. She had done everything required and she had held her determination close to her heart without giving any energy to doubt, or disappointment, or refusal. She had not been swayed by haters or naysayers or even those with titles who had laid down the law as to what was or was not going to happen.

With innocent conviction that the law of cause and effect was absolute and that with the right attitude and action ANYTHING is possible she had made the impossible possible.

She walked on that bus, threw her hands in the air and said, "told you!" As I watched the bus pull off, standing there with amazement I saw her press her hands against the window and mouth the words "Bye mom!"

When she returned her brother joined the Buddhist gymnastics group and her sister the age appropriate Young Pioneers group. I became a group leader, chanting with members who were facing obstacles and adversity, picking and dropping members off and attending meetings and lectures about the parables and principles of Buddhism. The four of us were at the center every chance we got. We would arrive and splinter into our respective meeting rooms where each could practice or learn what we came there for.

Within two months it seemed just a shift in focus had made it very clear. I didn't need alimony or staying married to someone who did not love me as I wanted to be loved. If I wanted the child support to come on time instead of months behind all the time then I needed to chant on it. If I wanted him to keep his word about visiting them then I needed to chant on it. If I wanted to heal our wounds and minimize our emotional damage then I needed to chant on it.

If they were still printing money we would get some. If fear would motivate or justify my choices then I would never find true happiness. I didn't need to hold on to a job that didn't pay that much or give me the flexibility and time I needed to raise my children. After all, child rearing is not a dress rehearsal. It's a time when once in a life time events happen every day and once missed, they are gone forever.

I needed to practice Buddhism sincerely, consistently, with devotion and then cast my net into the "field of infinite possibilities".

One night at dinner I said "I have an announcement. Today I quit my job." Instead of anyone being quiet or afraid they all cheered and said, "Great! That's great news. Mom is coming home."

Chapter Fourteen: Winter in Chicago

Guatama Buddha sat under the Bodhi tree the day he reached enlightenment, but before that moment of clarity and wisdom came, he was visited by demons and delusions (his own doubts) attempting to steer him off his path. If I just sit here without eating I will die. Should I get up? If I continue to sit here to solve the mystery of life and death won't everybody think I am crazy and even if I find the answer who can I tell it to?? Should I even be doing this? What difference is it going to make to anyone?

He pondered the mystery. If we are all human beings why are we not all the same? Some are healthy. Some are not. Some are rich. Some are poor. Some are one skin tone and others another. Why were we not all born the same?

Eventually when he had quieted his mind and refused to listen to his thoughts, he realized...Ah, we are each the accumulations of our thoughts, words, and deeds...none of which are extinguished by death but instead carried with us, engraved upon our lives from one life into the next. In time these accumulations came to be called karma. A thief in one lifetime may be born poor in another. Our causes from the past could explain our conditions in the present. While none of us remember our infinite past, it is always there.

I had no delusions that being a single mother without a job would be smooth sailing. My demons and delusions jolted me out of bed some days. Was I insane? What divorced single mother quits her job? What if we didn't make it and if we didn't wouldn't it be my fault?! I knew that I needed both time and money, but how to have both??

The school year was starting and the first thing I could do was volunteer at their schools. I could become a devoted parent volunteer and invest time in their interests.

Most urgent was sitting in on classes with my son. He was "acting out" in class, never turning in his homework, and generally daydreaming during the day. There was a "disconnect". When I talked to his teacher her response was "Well, if he does his work or doesn't do his work it doesn't matter. I'm just holding out until I can retire." Whoa!

Maybe she was burnt out but I could not be and I certainly could not afford to lose him to the typical path leading to juvenile incarceration and being a "drop out" so back to the "Jedi" story Phase II. I had to inject some "fun" into the days at school.

Before long all of the children in the class were more enthusiastic about school and hugging me good morning as they came in the classroom was a routine she couldn't stand. Oh well, treats, incentives, prizes, rewards, and loving to learn were their new expectations and they worked!

Just as I thought "whew!" got that back on the right track one night the house became icy cold. It was about 2 a.m. and we had been asleep for hours. Sure I was behind on the gas bill, but it was the dead of winter and by law the gas could not be turned off, right? Wrong. About midnight…and wait for it…on their dad's birthday, the gas had been turned off.

I bundled us all inside all the blankets and coats I could find until we could get out of there in the morning. With the children at school I raced to the gas company where they said there was no record of the gas being shut off but if it was it could

-101-

only be reconnected by them with payment in full. Not a possibility! Child support was our only source of income now and it was (like always) two months behind.

I was sitting in the house freezing when I heard a symphony of pop, bang, bong, pow....every radiator in the house cracked. The water left inside of them had frozen and the radiators just exploded.

It started on the first floor and as I ran from room to room I could see the ice through the cracks. There wasn't a radiator spared. The noises got so loud the whole house shook.

Uh uh, no, this can't be happening. I went from talking to the radiators to hugging them to a chuckle at the absurdity to the crazy laugh that took me to my knees. The laughter turned to tears to rocking back and forth to hallucinations about the ultimate defeat.

I'm not enough. I've never been enough and here is your proof. You blew it. Face it. You can't raise three children alone. When you have the money you don't have the time and when you make the time you don't have the money.

On my fifth attempt to reach their dad he answered the call. I told him what happened and that I just couldn't do it. Would he take them? Please at least take them now so they can have heat. He had remarried and he said he neither had room nor time to deal with three children. Besides there was no way his wife would approve. "Sounds like a personal problem to me" and that was it.

I called my folks who lived in St. Louis and told them both what had happened and what he said. My mom ended the call by saying "promise me you will NOT try to stay in that house tonight."

I packed a bag. Clothes for each of us for a week and when it was time to pick them up I put the suitcase in the car without a clue as to where we would go. I drove to his parents' house and told them the story. His dad said "he already called me and told me to expect you to show up." He was salty. His wife grabbed the bag and said "you guys can sleep in this room".

For months I met contractors at the house for estimates on what repairs would cost. My dad had said get estimates from contractors and I will figure it out. Almost every bid was unreasonable. It was

-103-

winter in Chicago. Supply and demand. It was cold and I was desperate. Some contractors said every pipe in the house would need to be replaced and the heating system converted to forced air and it just wasn't possible. The picture they painted was bleak.

In the mornings before school the children and I would do our morning prayers and after school we would go directly to the Buddhist Center for the evening prayers. We usually came back to their grandparents' home around 9 p.m. and then it was straight to bed.

I stayed away all day. After meeting contractors I was either at the library or at the center chanting or chanting with members in their homes. I went back to searching for jobs. I thought staying out would work out better as the children being talkative or playful or asking for things seemed disturbing and an extra uncomfortable reality for them.

Instead of that working I got a lecture one night from my former Father-in-law that what I needed in my life was God. The condition of my life was a direct result of me having turned my back on

God. The lecture turned into an argument and it was clear we had worn out our welcome.

The weather was warm enough that I thought it was time to return to the house so we did. Our routine continued as "normal" and then one saturday a man driving a van attached to a trailer of some sort pulled up on my front lawn. I ran outside to hail him down and ask if he had lost his mind! The driver jumped out and called out my name and said "Girl you sure look like your momma!"

Men jumped out of the van and the trailer with tools and supplies and said, "Well, let's get to work!" The sun was shining and the guys said, "Who is going to go get the beer?"

All of the contractors I had met had left me proposals for the work to be done which I had mailed to my parents who had in turn given them to their contractor friends. They had purchased all necessary supplies, hauled them from St. Louis and came ready to work. For three days the yard was filled with wood and pipes and debris and in their place were ducts and pipes for the new forced air heating system they installed. They worked long hours, talked only during breaks, of which there were few, and then slept in their trailer at night.

Before they left they made the gas bill current, tested the heating system, and the leader of the crew said, "Your parents really love you and your mom said to give you this note and for you to open it when we left. I remember when you were born and I feel like family because I almost married your aunt. Take good care of yourself and their grandkids and don't forget to read your mom's note."

Of course, the entire event left me speechless. I put the note on the altar because I wasn't sure if it was going to be the chastisement of the century or what. I just didn't know what to expect so I thought I will read it later. Much later.

Then when I closed the door and we had done our evening prayers I opened the note from my mom, which simply read, "You are enough."

Chapter Fifteen: The Exorcism

Life goes on. The seasons change. The wheel turns and cycles renew. With Christmas on the horizon I was torn between going to celebrate their tradition in St. Louis with family or focus energies on Buddhist ones. I was starting to think, "If I was a Muslim would they participate in Ramadan? Why am I continuing to participate in rituals that are not part of my faith?" Although now commercialized, Christmas was to be the celebration of the birth of the baby Jesus. I can celebrate his and any other birth, but the rituals attached to the current way it's done may not fit where I am trying to grow to.

My participation or non-participation was not related to judging what traditions worked for them, but my attempt to establish authenticity and integrity with myself. All part of my attempt to determine what worked for ME instead of folding into what expectations worked for others.

My mom saw Christmas as a time everybody packed up everything, no matter what was going on in their lives, and headed to her house to eat, talk, visit relatives and old friends, and generally be a part of the buzz at the residence. She loved having our old classmates come by to visit so she could catch up on their lives and feed them some of her home cooked food with a specialty of hers being German chocolate cake from scratch.

Finally I decided to send my three children but to experiment with not celebrating Christmas. Of course even Buddhist children want the gifts from under the tree so they were excited.

Three weeks before Christmas one of the guys from my Buddhist group and his girlfriend had been evicted. They were both working but still couldn't make ends meet and had gotten behind on the rent. He asked me if they could stay at my home for at least a month while they figured out what to do.

My girls agreed to double up in the same room for awhile so they moved in. About a week after they moved in they introduced us to their imaginary daughter who they claimed to see, but none of us could...or at least I couldn't. The children began to claim they saw her, too, so the entire shared living experience was interesting to say the least. Sure he had a little "mental karma", but didn't we all!

With the children leaving the Saturday before Christmas and because of the house guests I spent most of my time in my room with the door shut, reading, and writing or chanting at my altar. The house guests were Buddhists, too, so sometimes we all chanted together. On Christmas Eve the couple decided to go visit relatives.

With everybody gone I decided to go out one evening and while out I got into a conversation with a guy about Buddhism. We talked so long he asked me if I would like to go to the movies so we did. We left the movie, stopped by the liquor store, and then headed to my house. I thought what a nice unexpected day and date!

Things seemed fine and I called my mom to check on the children and say hi. I told her about my surprise date and she was not happy. "You took a strange man to your house?!" I wasn't concerned since I had houseguests and figured I wouldn't be home with him alone and then I would say good-night and that would be it for the date.

Several hours later my house guests had not returned but I kept expecting them any minute. Things seemed fine and then suddenly he snapped.

He got violent. He got angry. He got loud. I tried to calm him down and then I said you need to go now.

He grabbed me by my ankles and began to pull me towards the stairs. He had used the bathroom upstairs several times so he also knew the bedrooms were up there. The first set of stairs led to a landing and the second set of stairs led to the second floor.

The banister had slats of wood, which I kept clinging to one at a time without any traction. The first six steps, the landing, the second thirteen steps and then to the second floor and once he had me there he threw me on a bed and ripped off all my clothing. He took his off and said, "Bitch, this is what you deserve" and proceeded to beat and rape me for hours. Every time I thought he had fallen asleep I would try to sneak out of the bed and then he would repeat the beating and the rape. He kept shouting, "You're gonna have my baby you fucking Bitch!"

I kept thinking when are they going to put the key in the door! When are they going to come home?

Turns out the couple had decided to spend the night with relatives. There wasn't any way I could fight him off. He was tall. He was super strong. He was persistent. Just when I thought so this is how they will find me: raped, beaten and dead, I heard the front door open and the sound of the male friend calling out my name as he was ascending the stairs. Before he got to the second landing the guy had jumped into his clothes and darted down the stairs past my guest.

I sat up and wrapped myself in a sheet and crying, I tried to explain my story. We went to the emergency ward. With rape kit done and police report made, I overheard a nurse tell a staff person another holiday date-rape in room E.

Two days later it was time to head to the airport to retrieve the children. I took them home and listened to their stories about the holiday. Days later it was time for school. Each day was like any other. Taking them to school, looking for work, picking them up, preparing meals, listening to their stories about their days...old routines resumed.

Within a two weeks my breasts began to swell. I was pregnant. Within a week I called my mom to tell the story. Within two weeks she was there to take me to Planned Parenthood. As I lay there, legs spread, abortion in process I heard the doctor say to the nurse, "come here". What is it? They were talking about the fetus. He said, "I'm not sure what it is. I've never seen anything like it." "Can I see it?" "No, you cannot."

There was no time to grieve and who would I tell my story to? You met a guy you didn't know who you took home who raped you. Who would you want to tell that story to?

It took years, probably about a decade, to talk about it and then I found that just about every woman I spoke to about it had been raped. Karma? Of course, because everything is.

Eventually I began to write about it, talk about it, think it through, forgive myself without being jaded when it came to men or trusting people and now share it with you. Skeletons and clothes aren't the only things that come out of closets. Emotional baggage can get tucked away so long it screams to come out. I've gained more from speaking on it than I ever could have from stuffing it deep inside my soul.

Chapter Sixteen: The Second Time Around

Perhaps it's time to leave Chicago. Perhaps this was a place where no good things could find their way to me. Perhaps it would make more sense to be close to my family. Perhaps I could sell the house and leave this entire chapter behind. Perhaps.

I called a real estate agent who I had met in a previous house hunt. She came over and made an extensive list of repairs that would be necessary before she could even list it. All walls would need to be white. The floors would need to be sanded and varnished. The wood (and there was plenty of it) would need to be varnished. The exterior (stucco) would need to be painted and cracks repaired. It was all far more work than I could do alone, but if I could find someone to start the process perhaps in ninety days it would be presentable.

A member of the group I chanted with had the perfect guy for the job and he was looking for work. I made the call. He started immediately. Initially we seldom spoke while he worked all day. He was a perfectionist. For weeks he would arrive and work all day and into the evening. He was a Buddhist and take an occasional break to chant and go outside to smoke a cigarette. I asked upfront what deposit he needed and he said none and we could discuss his price after he was done if I was happy with his work.

A little uncomfortable with that I constantly asked him when he would need a payment. He constantly replied not to worry about the bill and that he wanted no payment until the job was done. I worried that his price would be ridiculously high and that I would be stuck with it if we never agreed on a fee. Nonetheless he refused to discuss money and only wanted supplies and cigarettes.

Eventually when he took his breaks to chant I would chant with him. We started talking about Buddhism. Several months had passed and more and more we discussed the philosophy and life. He had been a Buddhist nineteen years. I enjoyed the conversations and the house was beginning to be renewed.

Instead of ninety days the work was finished six months later and by then we were friends. Could we finally discuss a price?

Then he told me his story. He had discovered heroin after high school and when his habit got so bad that he was repeatedly arrested for stealing he had chanted to quit altogether. He would do fine for weeks, months, and even years, but he found that he did the worst when he had money. Money was not his friend because when he had it and had it predictably, he would always relapse.

He said he had been doing really well for two years but that he still didn't trust himself. I was so in love with the improvements on the house that I had decided not to sell. Throughout our conversations for half a year he had never revealed anything about himself and now I understood.

Actually "heroin" was just a word to me. I had never known anyone who had that habit or any addiction to any hard drugs. When he said he had a heroin habit it was like saying I once rode a bicycle. Naïve I had no fear. We aren't our past, right? We are works in progress and whatever wrongs we found or did or experienced were only to make us stronger. A survivor of my own tragedies and yet not feeling like a victim, I simply felt compassion and, in fact, a "good for you" attitude about the path he was on.

-115-

From August when the work on the house began to January when it ended I had enjoyed great conversations and hours of chanting with him and my house was looking pretty darn good. I was offered a job at a local university. Things were looking up. Whatever "issues" bubbled below the surface just got filed away in the "to be dealt with later" file.

The children were growing. Recitals, graduations, tournaments, contests, promotions from one grade to the next, before long a decade had passed since their dad and I broke up and since I don't expect "perfection" I was grateful for progress.

Their dad had remarried and had a son. They still had their visitation time with him. Trips out of town, outings, holiday gift giving…all of the rituals of them staying connected continued.

A guy I had once worked with had recon-nected to me and every Sunday we would go see a have dinner and see a play. Good food, conver-sation, and a social outing. It was a platonic relationship, but it was nice to get out and about. I was twenty years his junior and he was still smarting from a divorce.

One evening there was a knock at the door and the handyman who had restored my house was there. He didn't look like his calm and peaceful self. He looked nervous, agitated and he said he was having some problems and wondered if he could chant at my house. Sure. He came in and chanted about three hours. We picked up our "bible" of Buddhist gosho stories and said we will read whatever story we see first.

The "Dragon Gate" gosho was the one plucked from the chapters and we began to read. I would read a few paragraphs and then he would read a few.

In this particular gosho one learns about carp that swim upstream from a basin far below, seeking to ascend from the water below towards the ledge high above them. Swimming against the current, around, against and with predators and other carp seeking to also reach the top, these carp determine to fight the odds with a sense of urgency and mission to successfully achieve their goal. Those who succeed had a reward awaiting them.

They would transform from carp to dragons. From weaklings vulnerable to the vicissitudes of life as carp they would instead achieve prominence as strong, powerful, and commanding dragons.

Our spirits lifted from sharing this lesson on struggles in life, he asked me to help him start a search for a place to stay. Seems he and his mom had a falling out and he was suddenly homeless. We drove from place to place with the answer being consistently no. I frankly got tired of burning my gas, driving all over the city and when he asked at last if he could stay with me, my answer was only on one condition. We would have to get married for him to live at my house.

He said, "I am definitely not marriage material...already tried that once and I'm just no good at it." "Evidently", I said, "neither am I, but who knows perhaps we would transform from carp to dragons."

Without ever sharing a date, a kiss, a hug, or an outing, February 14, 1993 we married. We went from being friends to husband and wife, seeking to become partners and life mates as inseparable as fish and the water in which they swim.

"If you always do what you've always done you will always get what you always got." We announced the marriage to the children, we picked up his things and we both began the journey with the second time around and we began to chant.

Afterword

Needless to say my journey continues until today. Every person who has read this portion of it has shared in its energy and in this way invokes the questions we ponder about living, loving, and learning.

One married man I know said "Since I am married I never have to ask myself about my faults. My wife tells me of them constantly." Relationships empower us to question, to challenge, and to evolve as we define who we are and what we do. Even when we fumble and stumble as long as we learn and grow we can definitely capture the spirit of personal growth and development. Only arrogance and fear can keep us from this path. No matter what painful and/or joyful experiences we have along the way, the challenge is to stay the course, to persevere.

Love is well worth it all. At least for me it is.

In my sequel to this story, "Cattle Drive: A Relationship Safari" I share a collection of vignettes on dating experiences, including the subsequent ingredients of a second and third marriage. Through blog postings, workshops on personal development and spiritual growth I continue to invite others to step into their space where they can see their choices more clearly; thereby, making self responsibility empowering.

Whether we find peace at the mosque, the temple, the center, the cathedral, the church, or in our living rooms, peace is the ultimate companion piece to self fulfillment.

For information on Nichiren Buddhism and locations in one's area for local events, literature, and resources, please check: www.sgi-usa.org.

Additional information on books written by Dr. Johnson can be found at:
http://mcintoshandshobeyassociates.weebly.com
where you can complete the contact form to request information on book signing parties, book clubs, and workshops offered by this author and publisher. We can respond to your questions and needs after hearing from you.

Namaste!

About the Author:

Victoria L. Johnson is a social scientist with a Ph.D. in Political Science from Tufts University in Medford, Massachusetts. While completing her doctorate at Tufts she was simultaneously a Fellow at the Harvard Program for Science and International Affairs (PSIA) which is now part of the Harvard University Kennedy School of Government. Pergamon Press published portions of her dissertation on "Brazilian Nuclear Development: Intent and Capabilities" that was the result of field research in Brazil funded by the Ford Foundation.

As a Consultant to The Division of Energy and Environmental Systems (EES) of Argonne National Laboratory, she served on an interdisciplinary team of specialists for The United States Department of Energy investigating nuclear waste contamination at the Kerr-McGee Nuclear Plant in West Chicago, IL.

As a Professor of Political of Political Science at Loyola University, Chicago State University and University of Illinois at Chicago (UIC) she specialized in comparative politics, International Security, Nuclear Development and Non-

-122-

proliferation. As a "Diversity Consultant" for the Association of Junior Leagues she trained the membership and Board of Directors on cultural literacy, recruitment and retention.

After forming her own consulting firm, McIntosh & Shobey Associates in 1986 she provided training, program development, and strategic planning assistance to national and non-profit agencies committed to diversity, the implementation of policy initiatives, and community development for non-profit organizations committed to civic engagement, advocacy, and the advancement of working families.

In 2003 she relocated from Chicago to Philadelphia where she used her skills with constituency and coalition building to organize community empowerment and educational reform initiatives that she wrote about in her book: "The Bad Lands at a Good Time: a look at neighborhood revitalization in North Philadelphia".

In addition to her professional endeavors, she wrote several books.

"Family Trees with Broken Branches: a search for the treasures of the heart" was written after providing hospice care for her terminally ill parent and the shifts his death created in family relations.

"When There Are No More Tears: A Buddha's Story of Love" is an autobiographical story of her first marriage, divorce, experiences with single parenting, and personal development.

"Cattle Drive: the relationship Safari" is an autobiographical story of her second and third marriages, as well as vignettes on dating.

"A Life Sabbatical" is a collection of prose and poetry written 2003-2012 during almost a decade of personal transformation.

Her mother gave her a journal when she was seven and has since been writing inspirational non-fiction stories about her own life and those of others seeking personal development.

Despite her numerous professional accomplishments, she considers parenting and motherhood her most important activity of her life.

For further information or her assistance see:
http://mcintoshandshobeyassociates.weebly.com